Task Management:

Checklist and Self Discipline for Personal Success

Darlene Tucker

2018

Text Copyright © Darlene Tucker

All rights reserved. No part of this guide may be reproduced in any form without permission in writing from the publisher except in the case of brief quotations embodied in critical articles or reviews.

ISBN-13: 978-1717102768

ISBN-10: 171710276X

Legal & Disclaimer

The information contained in this book and its contents is not designed to replace or take the place of any form of medical or professional advice; and is not meant to replace the need for independent medical, financial, legal or other professional advice or services, as may be required. The content and information in this book has been provided for educational and entertainment purposes only.

The content and information contained in this book has been compiled from sources deemed reliable, and it is accurate to the best of the Author's knowledge, information and belief. However, the Author cannot guarantee its accuracy and validity and cannot be held liable for any errors and/or omissions. Further, changes are periodically made to this book as and when needed. Where appropriate and/or necessary, you must consult a professional (including but not limited to your doctor, attorney, financial advisor or such other professional advisor) before using any of the suggested remedies, techniques, or information in this book.

Upon using the contents and information contained in this book, you agree to hold harmless the Author from and against any damages, costs, and expenses, including any legal fees potentially resulting from the application of any of the information provided by this book. This disclaimer applies to any loss, damages or injury caused by the use and application, whether directly or indirectly, of any advice or information presented, whether for breach of contract, tort, negligence, personal injury, criminal intent, or under any other cause of action.

You agree to accept all risks of using the information presented inside this book.

You agree that by continuing to read this book, where appropriate and/or necessary, you shall consult a professional (including but not limited to your doctor, attorney, or financial advisor or such other advisor as needed) before using any of the suggested remedies, techniques, or information in this book.

Table of contents

Introduction	5
Why Should You Create A To-Do List?	6
Why the System Fails	15
The most popular list systems	22
Characteristics of To-Do List	27
Methods of Reference	31
Prioritize your To-Do List	35
Get Started	39
Rules of Compilation	42
Ten strategies of building the to-do list	45
Conclusion	61

Introduction

Are there times you feel overpowered by the number of things you have to do? Do you miss due dates frequently while overlooking essential errands and assurances you made to individuals, that are critical for your business life? Are you under the impression that you have no influence over the things in your life? Is this how you feel most of the time?

These are all symptoms of something that can be traced back to most of us: not having a plan for the day or in simpler terms, not having a to-do list.

You will soon find that this book will guide you to enhance your own effectiveness and efficiency using a to-do list. Here you will also find out about the connection between individual productivity and individual efficiency, and additionally, how to enhance the latter using a to-do list. If the information contained in this guide is utilized the measure of stress in your life will be lessened significantly as you quit missing deadlines, quit breaking promises you make, and understand the things that are occurring in your life.

Is it safe to say that you are prepared to master the art of crafting a to-do list to improve your own productivity and efficiency towards a superior personal satisfaction and quality life? Assuming this is the case, how about we proceed!

Why Should You Create A To-Do List?

You have a lot of things to do, yet you do not know how or where to start? Don't worry; it is not the end of the world. What you need to do is create a to-do list that in turn will help you sort out your work and get every single item in your list done.

Essentially, a to-do list is just a list of things that you have to do, especially if there are an overwhelming number of things that you need to accomplish. A to-do list (TDL) is a list of prioritized tasks that you need to finish. It lists all the stuff you need to accomplish with the most important ones populating the upper area of your list and the least important ones occupying the lower area. Since you have a lot of things to do, you will most likely lose track of these things. As a result, you tend to forget to do the other things or focus more on one task while neglecting other tasks that require attention too. Therefore, you need to create a to-do list to keep track of your work and make sure that you can get all of it done in a timely and professional manner

> **Essentially, a to-do list is just a list of things that you have to do.**

A TDL helps you focus by organizing the things you need to do so you can see the big picture of your schedule for a particular period of time (daily, weekly, or monthly) as well as detailed lists of what you need to accomplish and have already accomplished. Using a TDL enables you to organize by listing down all your scheduled tasks in one place, minimizing the chances of you forgetting something important. And by listing them in order by importance or urgency, you are able to focus on what the things that are most urgent and important and leave the least urgent and important ones for later.

You'll need to use a TDL if you want to avoid being overloaded with too many tasks, be it business or personal. Think of a TDL as a car's fuel gauge – it tells the driver how much gasoline is left in the tank so you'll know if you'll need to gas up on the way to your destination or not. In a similar way, your TDL acts like a task gauge, helping you monitor your schedule and decide whether or not you are able to accept more responsibilities, tasks, or errands. Not using a TDL can wreak havoc on your schedule and subject you to a lot of stress. Using one can help you manage your life much better and minimize (or even eliminate) stress.

So you are asking why on earth you even have to create a to-do list. You may feel like you are only giving yourself an extra work since you first have to create a to-do list when you can start working on the task itself. Is a to-do list even necessary? The answer is YES. To help you fully appreciate the importance of a to-do list, listed below are some of the major perks:

1. It helps you organize your tasks. One of the main reasons why you can't get your work done is that you do not know where to start. You feel that everything is too cluttered and needs organization. Therefore, with the help of a to-do list, you will be able to organize your tasks. You can easily point out which one you should prioritize and address first.

2. It prevents you from forgetting the work that you need to do. We all know that not everyone is gifted with a sharp memory. Most of us have the tendency to forget things from time to time. We tend to forget where we have placed our keys, let alone every task that we have on our agenda. If you create a to-do list, however, you will most likely not forget the things that you need to do, since you can easily be reminded of them just by looking at your list.

3. It helps you to be more productive. Again, we tend to procrastinate because we are overwhelmed by the number of tasks that we need to do. We also prioritize the things that we like more than the things that are of primary importance. However, when you create a to-do list, you will be able to identify which things are needed to be done immediately and which are of less importance and can wait. Moreover, with a to-do list, you can see how many tasks are already done and how many are still left, which in turn helps you know if you need to work fast or if you still have enough time to move at a comfortable pace.

4. It keeps you motivated to get everything done. Many believe that a to-do list is an effective motivational tool since it helps you clarify and pinpoint your goals. For example, if your goal for today is to "be productive," then you will most likely not achieve your goal because (i) it is too vague and general and (ii) you do not know how exactly you should start in order to be productive. With your to-do list, you can easily identify short-term goals which are relatively easier to achieve and motivating enough to keep you going. If your goals for today are to clean your room, your house, and your car, write your essay, and go grocery shopping you will most likely achieve your goals because you know exactly what you need to do and what you want to achieve by the end of the day. Isn't it motivating enough to tick some items off your to-do list and see that you are progressing?

With To-Do List, you will surely have an organized life.

Before I introduce you to the various strategies that will bring order and peace to your life, I feel that it would be better for you to have a glimpse of the many benefits of having an organized life.

You might have been thinking about fixing this part of your life, but did not have a clue on where or how to begin. This book is a great first step! It acts as a guide on how to make the first move towards the fulfillment of a stress-free and organized life. I will share the strategies which will be discussed later in this book to better organize areas in your life that need a little sprucing up.

For now, we need to motivate you to get started on having a clutter-free life; we will have a look at several benefits of being organized. You might wonder what the point of having an organized life is. You might enjoy just throwing things all over the place or not having to put in the work to get things put away at the end of the day. If you are wondering why you should choose to live an organized life, there are a lot of great benefits to doing it. Below are just some of them:

Save Money

One of the first benefits of having a more organized life is that you will be able to save money. How can you save money by being more organized? For one, think of the many times you've found yourself rummaging through your mail only to find overdue bills! Being late on the bills is going to cost you a lot of money in late fees, and just by having a more organized life, you will be able to put the bills in a place where you can find them and pay them on time, thus saving money. An organized office or home will have all the bills in one place and arranged according to which bills need to be paid first. If you do this, you will never miss a bill! On the other hand, if mail is all over the place, bills might be buried or misplaced. By the time you realize they're due it will already be too late to pay them, and you'll have to pay penalties and other fees as well. Imagine all that avoidable cost you could save if you only organized your mail.

Another massive benefit of being organized is that you can

save money on daily expenses. You can plan your meals ahead of time, you can budget well, and know all the things that you need to buy at the grocery store. You won't need to make several stops because you forgot stuff. If you are able to put a list of the things that you need together before you head out, you can avoid having to go to the store every day of the week or several times in the same day. This is going to save you a lot of time, as well as the money that you would be spending on the gas to go back and forth. In addition, if you are like most people, each time you go to the store you will find something else that you would like to buy, whether or not you really need it, and you might end up purchasing it. You could save money by not going as much and not putting yourself in a position to be tempted. Besides that, if you are not organized it is very easy to buy an item only to realize that you had one already stashed somewhere at home.

Another way that being organized will save you money is that you will be able to take advantage of any of the discounts or promotions that come your way. If you want to start couponing or getting preferred customer rewards at a store that you like, organizing the paperwork for this will save you the money that you need in the long run. When papers are misplaced because you are not organized, it can end up leading to disaster, and this means you will miss out on a lot of the great opportunities that could be saving you money.

> **One of the first benefits of having a more organized life is that you will be able to save money.**

You might also find better deals on trips and other vacations that you would like to go on. You will be able to take the time to look around at different sites and ask the right questions, bookmark the sites that you need, and get everything organized without spending more on the trip or misplacing things while having to spend extra at the last minute. There are just so many things that you will be able to save money on as long as you are able to stay as organized as possible.

Save Time

The next benefit of learning how to organize your life is that you will gain a lot more time. Imagine all the time you waste digging through heaps of stuff just to find your keys or credit card. Think about all of the time that you are wasting at work trying to find that report that your boss sent, or getting everything organized and ready to go before you are even able to start on the work that you need to do. Before I began organizing my life, there was a time I spent a whole hour looking for my car keys. I ended up being late for my doctor's appointment and that meant I had to reschedule, which was several weeks ahead! And how could I forget the missed appointment with my client that nearly cost me my entire career? Time really is money.

An organized person not only has everything they need on hand, they can also find stuff much faster. When they are looking for something, they know where it is right away and are able to go and pick it up without a problem. They are not wasting all of this time trying to find it because they already know where it is. They are not wasting tons of hours each week looking for things that they need; things that are not really that important but which they need nonetheless. They are able to find what they need in just seconds and then get on with the other stuff that they have to do. The bottom line is, it is much better when you know where to find everything you need so you don't waste time trying to find stuff.

Increase Productivity

Being organized also helps you become more efficient in what you do. I also feel less stressed (and more proud) when I schedule activities and get them done on time. When you organize activities, you can weed out unimportant stuff and work more efficiently. You will be able to avoid stress, and you will feel a sense of achievement when your life becomes more manageable as well.

If you can get organized, you will be able to find everything that you need right away, which will save you money right from the beginning. You can get to work immediately from the start and avoid the distractions that come from spending all that time looking for things. If you do find that you are missing something and need to grab it, you can just reach right over to it and continue working, avoiding the distraction, loss of focus, and the time that it is going to take in order to find the item. This can save you hours during the day that you never realized were wasted and soon you will be getting so much more done than ever before. Think of all that free time you will have at the end of the day; you might even be able to go home on time and spend some time with your family rather than working another late night.

More importantly, all the time that you save by being organized can be used for other important things that you have always wanted to do but never seemed to have time for.

Have you been yearning to start surfing or cooking lessons, but never have the time? You may need to organize your life in order to have extra time and do more of the things that you love.

Reduce Stress

You might not have thought of this, but having a more organized life will reduce the stress that you are feeling. Most people think that being organized is more stressful and they would rather be more laid back and not have to worry about keeping things organized. This is a harmufl attitude to have. Think about it; how many times have you been stressed out because you couldn't find something when you were in a hurry and needed to get to work or to an appointment? How many times were you worried about how things would turn out at work or school because you were not able to find an important paper or something else that was needed? If you think back, there are probably quite a few times like that, and you might have had a lot of instances where losing things and being disorganized was actually stressing you out more than you could imagine. Now think about how it would be if you were more organized in your life. You are able to find all of your papers, the keys never get lost again, and everything is exactly in the place that it should be. This does not mean that you have to get obsessive about it, but having a good system of organization in your life can make all of the difference.

There is nothing worse than the feeling of not having control over your life. This is exactly how you'll feel when you have a disorganized lifestyle. Can you imagine coming home to a house where the bills and the children's toys are all over the place, where even finding a place to sit is impossible? Worse still, you may move to the kitchen and find utensils and dirty dishes all over the counters.

Now, imagine walking into a nice home where everything is where it is supposed to be, and you do not end up tripping over toys all over the place. From experience, I know it feels much better and lighter when you come home to a clean and organized place. It even helps you relax!

Feel Empowered

When your life gets more organized, you will feel a surge of confidence, pride, and self-esteem. Think of how great it is going to be when you can tell everyone that you got the project done on time or even earlier than anticipated. Think of how great it is going to feel when your boss asks you for a report, or something else, and you are able to just grab it rather than telling them that you will retrieve it later. Imagine how great it is going to feel when you are able to have people over because you do not have to worry about how messy your place looks. You will not even have to shy away from inviting friends to your house, because you are no longer ashamed of any mess or clutter. If you have an organized home, you will be more than happy to host guests and feel a sense of pride when they leave your home after having a great time.

All of this is going to empower you to feel so much better

about yourself. Those who are disorganized might like to pretend that they are easygoing and really laid-back, but in reality, they are a big mess and might be wondering how to get everything done each day. They might even be wondering how others are able to remain so cool and collected. Now it is your turn to be calm and collected by getting everything in order and enjoying all that life has to offer with the feeling of empowerment.

Achieve Goals

If you want to achieve your goals, you need to eliminate the barriers that are preventing you from doing what you have to. Oftentimes, it is important that all your life processes are streamlined to enable you have maximum focus on the effort, resources and time towards your objectives. Having a cluttered way of life will make you use up more energy than is needed. This will make achieving goals much more difficult.

The benefits that you can enjoy by organizing your life are limitless! Let's start organizing!

Why the System Fails

When creating their own to-do lists, most people tend to just put whatever they want to include in the list without ever putting that much thought into it. They keep on writing down everything—their tasks, projects, appointments, and everything that they want to do. However, the problem usually is that they don't clearly see the things or actions that need to be done.

It is easy for us to make this kind of mistake with our to-do lists. There is no need to worry, though. The key to an effective to-do list as well as daily action is identifying what mistakes you usually make and then find ways on how you will be able to correct these mistakes.

Here are the most common mistakes that people usually do whenever they are creating their to-do lists, as well as the best ways to fix these mistakes:

Writing Lists That are too Long

If simplicity is the key to creating an effective to-do list, then it is only obvious that overstuffing it will have just the opposite effect. You need to understand that one task is not the same as the other task. Each one of them has its own characteristics, and they vary depending on the amount of time and preparation they need, as well as the task's importance (i.e., whether it is urgent or not).

Now when planning out our schedule for the day, we always have this tendency to include in our list even the tiniest details of our tasks. We write down everything, which results in having a lengthy list. We usually mix all of our tasks into a single list, regardless whether they differ in time, preparation, or importance. Little did we know that this kind of list is usually "demotivating," because we feel like there are too many things to do. We simply can't accomplish all the items that are included in these types of lists.

In order to overcome this mistake, you always have to keep in mind that your to-do list should be as brief as possible. Write less than 5 important tasks that you want to accomplish for the day. Prioritize the tasks and sort them according to their importance. For example, writing an essay which is due the next day is a task that is more important than let's say, arranging your shelf. Since you want to accomplish these tasks today, you will put them both in your to-do list. However, you need to put "Write my Essay" on the top of your list since it is more important than your other tasks.

Once you are done with your top priority, you can now move on to your second priority, and then on the third, until you have already ticked everything off your list.

Just remember that while it is important that you plan everything, it may not be that helpful if you are going to start your day with a very lengthy to-do list. This will only make you feel like you have too many tasks to do when in fact you really don't. Instead, focus more on few specific tasks that you can easily handle.

Having an Ambiguous List

One thing that also makes you refrain from following your to-do list is the fact that the list itself is too vague for you to see the beginning or the endpoint of everything. More often than not, we can't accomplish our tasks because we do not even know how to start. This in turn only causes stress and will not in any way motivate us to do something.

For example, doing your household chores is too ambiguous of an idea to include on your to-do list. Yes, you want to do household chores today, but how exactly are you going to do that? How are you even going to start? There are a lot of household chores: washing the dishes, doing the laundry, sweeping and then mopping the floor, and many more. Which one are you going to do first? Which one are you going to do next?

> **We usually mix all our tasks in a single list, regardless whether they differ in time, preparation, or importance**

So instead of writing "Do the household chores," list the more specific and actionable tasks, such as "Wash the dishes," or "Do the laundry, or "Wash the car" and so on. Keep in mind though that you should not make your list too long, or else it will be a lot harder for you to finish.

Just keep in mind that your task should have specific course of action for you to know if you are already done with that task or not. Moreover, each task must also have a measurable outcome. It should also be simple enough to be done in a single time frame. Lastly, your task should also include a well-defined endpoint.

Poor Time Management

Planning out the things that you need to accomplish does not only mean that you know what tasks you need to do. It also means that you know how long it will take you to complete each task. For instance, if you know that writing a presentation will take you several hours, you should not t put it off until the very last minute.

More often than not, we usually just write down the things that we have to accomplish without really knowing how much time we need to devote for each task. Sometimes we keep on doing things that only require a few moments of our time first, and then we tend to delay those tasks that require more time until n we no longer have enough time.

Our productivity is at stake when we do not know how to manage out time properly. So before you even start doing any task, you first have to roughly estimate the amount of time that each task may require. Doing so will help you come up with a simple framework, or at least an idea of which task you can complete within a particular day.

You do not have to worry if your rough estimate is wrong (that is why it is called an estimate), what's more important is that you at least know which task you have to prioritize given its possible time requirement. Eventually, you will start learning how to manage your time properly. ince developing this habit will require practice and effort, you have to do this on a regular basis until you get used to it. Afterwardyou will no longer notice how much you have improved at predicting how many tasks you can actually do in a day and how much time each task will need.

It Doesn't Account for Time

I hate to break it to you, but there are only 24 hours in a day. Subtract the time that you are asleep and at work, and you are only left with about 8 hours in the best case scenario. If you have a family the amount of time left is even less. Between making dinner, picking up kids from school, and working on school projects, you are barely left a few hours to relax and enjoy your self.

So, if you put 20 items on your list without considering the time that it will take for you to finish them, you will most likely end up scratching your head trying to figure out why you haven't even completed a quarter of them. When tomorrow begins and you have even more chores, you will find yourself feeling too overwhelmed, tearing your to-do list into a million pieces.

Being Derailed by Random and Unexpected Things

We do not always have control over the things that are going to happen every day. It is true that every day is totally random and different from other days. There will always come a time when we will experience emergencies and other unexpected toccurences. When these things just fall into our laps, we can't do anything but adjust.

It is not just us who need to adjust though; our schedule should reflect that. We should plan out the structure of our day in such a way that it is flexible enough to adjust in different circumstances.

Start your day with a look on your calendar. Check your schedule to see what activities or tasks you have for that particular day. Take a look at your future schedules as well. You should now have an idea what your day is going to be like. When it comes to making your schedule flexible, it does not necessarily mean that you should change the way you have planned out your day just to make adjustments for unexpected things. It only means that you should have at least one hour of vacant time every day to make room for unexpected tasks.

So when you are creating a to-do list for the day, make sure that you do not occupy every hour of the entire day for the planned activities. Make sure that you still have free hours to adjust for emergencies. If there isn't any work that comes your way, you can still make use of your free time to relax and give yourself a quick break.

Having the Mindset that Only on Small Outcomes

While it is important that you prioritize urgent tasks, it is also important that you think about your long-term plans. Are these urgent tasks that prove valuable in the long run?

When it comes to creating your to-do list, you should not only focus on what is urgent. You must also consider those things that have the biggest effect on your long-term goals. For instance, you should add into your to-do list "Do research for my upcoming presentation." This presentation may not be as urgent as the other items on your to-do list (such as let's say, attending an important meeting), but at least you are already preparing for it little by little so that it won't pile up by the last minute. It is important that you take a look into the "bigger picture," because the more you do so, the more you will most likely achieve.

Having no Connection Between Your Tasks and your Goals

In everything that we do, it is important that we always think about our goals. Our goals are the ones which will keep us motivated to continue working on our tasks no matter how stressful they can be. Once you know your goal for doing this particular thing, you will then find yourself extremely excited to start working on it.

> **It is still important to keep in mind that your life does not depend solely on your to-do list.**

Before anything else, you first need to clearly identify your reason for including a particular task on your list. If you put that item there just because you feel like it is something that you need to do, then think about adding in that item again. Make sure that each task on your list should serve you a purpose. The more it is connected with your long-term goals, the more you will get motivated and excited to work on it, and get it done.

Worrying too Much About your Incomplete to-do List

As what was discussed in the previous chapter, it is important that you keep four lists of activities that you need to accomplish. These lists include tasks that should be done immediately as well as tasks that can still be delayed for a later time. These are also the ones that will help you stay productive and do more.

However, it is still important to keep in mind that your life does not depend solely on your to-do list. If you do not get to tick off every single item on your list, don't agonize over it. You may still have the time to do the remaining tasks the next day. That is why you need to prioritize doing the most important tasks on your list. Once you have already done them, at least you can now say that you have already accomplished something for the day.

The most popular list systems

There are several to-do list systems that people tend to use. You just apply one that suits your tastes and ensures that you obtain maximum benefits from it. Here are some of the popular list systems.

1. GTD (Getting Things Done). GTD is a framework that one uses to organize and track their projects and tasks. The aim is to ensure that you apply 100% trust in the system which you use to collect your tasks, available ideas, and the projects at hand (just everything). It is built on five pillars:

    a. Capturing everything (ideas, recurring tasks, everything you want to do)

    b. Organizing them into categories and order of priority.

    c. Reflect on the list you have created

    d. Engage and execute the steps.

2. Zen to Done (ZTD). It is a powerful and simple system that helps you develop the good habits that ensure your tasks and projects are organized, your day is structured and simple, your space is clean and clear of any clutter, which helps you to concentrate on what you ought to be doing here and now, and avoid distractions. It addresses problems noted in GTD like

    a. While the GTD is a series of changes in your habits

at a time, ZTD focuses on a single habit at any given time.

b. GTD focuses more on the capture and process stages than the doing stage. ZTD places much focus on the actual doing

c. GTD lacks structure while ZTD has the plan habit that addresses the "Most Important Things" and a sequence of completing the tasks.

d. GTD has too much to be done that can stress you out. ZTD is focused on how to simplify the tasks by importance

3. Mind Maps. A mind map is a system aimed at streamlining your day and increasing productivity through connecting a number of dependencies on a given task. You may have your tasks split in accordance to context like pay, go to, or lunch and make them the primary nodes. You can start by creating/writing down your activities, establishing the central theme, connect the general associations, and apply the W-questions like what to pay, who to pay, where to pay, which other things, etc. You can also use the day as the central idea and the tasks or projects as the main branches which can be subdivided into smaller branches

4. Bullet Journal. This is to-do list system in which the tasks or projects are recorded using bullet points as the main or core structure. It has four key sections that include:

   a. Index that includes page numbers for all topics and sections.

   b. Future Log that contains the tasks that one needs to undertake in the future.

c. Monthly Log that contains all the calendar events and the to-do lists for the month.

d. Daily Log that has the daily activities

e. The 1-3-5 Rule. Here, you choose one huge task, three tasks that are medium-sized, and five considerably smaller tasks to complete in a given day. This system is flexible, encourages you to focus on high-value tasks and eliminates over-optimism.

Types

I know that at least once in your entire life, you must have tried creating a to-do list. You have written down every single thing that you need to accomplish for the day. You have allotted a specific time for each task and you have already scheduled which item should be done first and which ones can still be put off at a later time. However, while you have already had everything planned out, you still find yourself struggling to finish your tasks. You then realize that at the end of the day, it is still somewhat hard for you to accomplish anything.

Why is that so, you ask? That is because you always tend to take the so-called "scattershot" approach when it comes to planning your schedule and to-do list. You include everything that you want to add in your list. You even include those emergency tasks and deadlines, which only add to the pile of chores that you have to accomplish. This, of course, leads to an overwhelming list of tasks that already seem hard for you to do.

You may have already given up creating a to-do list because you find it ineffective. However, it is not the to-do list that is ineffective, per se, but rather it is the way you created it. Always keep in mind that one task is different from the other. There are tasks that need to be done as soon as possible, while there are some that need a detailed action plan and therefore require a much longer time period. There are also some that can still wait until you already have the free time to do them.

Now, your to-do list may seem ineffective because you tend to pile all of these tasks in just one list. If you want an effective to-do list, then it is about time that you know how to sort out your tasks so that they will not pile up in just a single list. In order for you to come up with a helpful to-do list, you have to clearly identify the tasks that you need to do within days, weeks, and months. Once you have already identified the weight of your work depending on the amount of time that each requires, you need to create four different kinds of to-do list, so that you will no longer have to put all of them together in a single list.

Here are the four types of to-do list and what each is for:

1. Idea capture list

This list serves as your "dumping ground" for each idea that you want to accomplish or achieve in the near future. This list includes both tasks that can be acted upon immediately as well as those that still need a deliberate action plan. The purpose of creating an idea capture list is for you to develop that habit of adding new items to this list every day as well as check it for at least once in a week.

2. Project list

A project list, on the other hand, includes tasks that require more than two separate actions. Basically, you include in this list the tasks that you need to do in order to fulfill the idea that you want to achieve someday (which you may have written in your idea capture list).

3. Weekly task list

The weekly task list, as the term itself implies, include those task that you need to put in your weekly schedule. It is usually a combination of personal as well as professional duties that you have to accomplish within a particular week.

Since it is a list of your weekly tasks, you have to divide your work among the days of the week. It does not necessarily mean that you divide them into seven equal parts (since one week is comprised of seven days); you just have to plan which tasks need to be done on Monday, or on Tuesday, and so on. Therefore, you need to have a general list of your work that you need to accomplish within this week. Write them down altogether without thinking first whether one is more important than the other; the idea is just that you need to see exactly what tasks are waiting to be done.

Once you have already listed the tasks that you need to accomplish, it is now the right time to group them according to their deadlines. For example, if your report needs to be handed in by Wednesday, you would not schedule working on that by Thursday. You would put that task on Monday, or even on Tuesday (as long as you still have enough time).

4. Most important things (MITs)

Lastly, this list is the group of tasks that need to be done as soon as possible. These are the tasks that can no longer wait and are more important than the other chores that you have on your list.

Usually, MITs are just a small list, which include the set of tasks that you have to prioritize within a particular day. MITs usually include about less than five tasks only. The idea of creating an MIT is that you need to know which tasks you should prioritize and do first before working on any other tasks. As we all know, we procrastinate because we tend to do other things instead of those that need to be accomplished immediately. But with the help of your MIT, you can clearly identify which tasks you have to do now so that your attention will no longer be directed upon the less important things.

Characteristics of To-Do List

Most of us have our own styles of to-do lists, but organizational experts have discovered that some ways of putting an effective list together are better than others.

Nonetheless, there are common characteristics of all good to-do lists that contribute to our productivity and reduce our stress.

Here are ten characteristics of the best to-do lists, gleaned from research about hundreds of lists over the years, and the latest literature and science on the subject.

Serious preparation work

The most effective to-do lists start with you taking a brief time out to write down all the tasks that you need to complete. If you want to emulate this, pick a specific time period for your planning. Many business people like to plan per quarter of the year; others live their lives according to seasons. Still others prefer just to look a month ahead, and others a week. Estimates are that to do this part of the list-making like the pros, it will take you between one and two hours.

Task breakdown

Once the tasks are all laid before you, study them to see what's involved. Are they one-act tasks, or complicated, multi-facetedtasks. If they fall into the latter class, then they need to be broken down into as many small steps as possible.

Specific details

For example, the agenda of the very effective list writer does not say "Meet with Jack at 9 a.m. It says "meet with Jack, bring coffee, cream, no sugar, and persuade him to sign off on his website content. Negotiate at least three weeks more in timing before a prototype of the site needs to be shown."

Prioritization

We tend to think of prioritization as numbering 1, 2 and 3 and so on, and while that is essential for daily lists, for a longer term list it is sometimes more useful to simply designate whether the task is urgent or essential but not urgent, or needed but neither urgent nor essential. Just using your own code or the initials U, I, and NU would work.

Adaptability to your life

This is a very controversial area when it comes to list making. Science supports that short daily lists with no more than three to four items are most effective for the majority of people. But when it comes to your own life, don't be governed by other people's rules. Figure out what works best for you. Many managers who must stay on top of a multitude of projects find that having a longer list that ensures some progress is made daily. is more stress-reducing than having to select just three projects a day to work on.

> **Short daily lists with no more than three to four items are most effective for the majority of the people.**

Advance planning

A common characteristic of effective to-do listers is their insistence of never ending one day without planning the next. You may decide that marking off your priorities for the next day is something that closes your day well for you in your workplace, or you may find your ability to make decisions and focus more keenly comes after you've reached the quiet point of your evening. Whatever system works best for you is fine. Either way, you will find your morning gets started more effectively if you ensure that your priority list is completed and waiting for you when you awaken.

Choice of paper or technology

This again is a matter of personal choice. Many people who use the traditional list writing skill of pen to paper feel a sense of calmness and control infused in them as they go through their daily listing exercise. Others find it much more efficient to use even a simple Microsoft Word document list or one of the many other electronic options from "Evernote" to "Toodledo" to "Remember the Milk".

Unique solutions

A president or prime minister, for example, has a far larger list of projects to keep moving along than the average person. They may need more complex technical programs that do some of their scheduling and send them alerts frequently. If your life has become unbearably complicated, consider seeking organizational solutions that are customized for your situation.

Transitioning across life's borders

Our average days are usually a blend of what we do for ourselves and for others. We move seamlessly through the art of handling our own personal grooming, making breakfast for ourselves and others, picking up a colleague and heading to work, completing our work tasks, remembering to call midway through the day to check on a sick friend, meeting a colleague for lunch, and rushing home a half-hour early to be there for the air conditioning service technician.

What distinguishes the to-do list of really effective people is their acknowledgment that our lives must move effortlessly through various segments to blend into a whole. Instead of handling only work tasks, they also jot down their other key appointments, understanding that for life to operate smoothly, we must be able to integrate all of its parts.

Personalized techniques

List-making, as those who do it can effectively confirm, is primarily the art of remembering what needs to be done, deciding what is most important, and then completing the tasks at hand. Many people report that the most challenging aspects of the three pillars of list-making is making the decision about what is most important.

Some people develop unique techniques to help them decide what should be number one on their list. They ask themselves: Which item on my list, if not completed today, is going to cause me the most grief later on? Others ask which task has the most revenue associated with it, or the most warmth of personal accomplishment. Create your own assessment system based on your own values and you will find the decision becomes much easier.

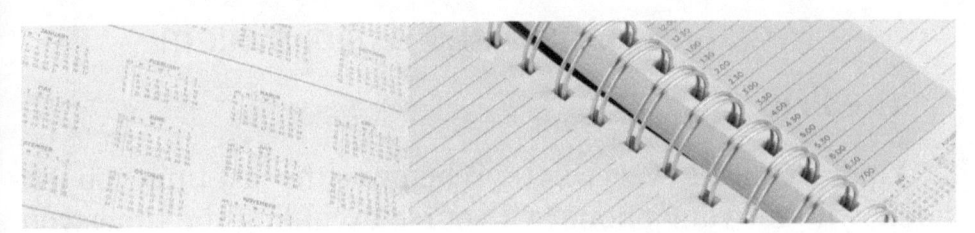

Methods of Reference

We are going to figure out which to do list system is better for your productivity, digital or paper. And to do that, we are going to look at the pros and cons of both.

Pros and Cons of the Paper System

The Pros

The paper system is practically unlimited. You can transform it, you can draw any type of shape on it, and you can do whatever you want with it. You can't do that with a digital to-do list application. Though the writing process may be slower, you actually get to engrain more information when taking down your tasks on paper.

How about just crossing completed tasks off your to-do list paper? You love it right? I love it too. It always gives me a sense of accomplishment.

Finally, the paper doesn't run out of power. You don't have to worry about your device dying.

The Cons

If you ever get a little to-do list planner or something, you would agree with me that it can get lost.

A paper planner can be bulky and it may be inappropriate to go everywhere with your paper to-do list in hand. But you can take your phone everywhere with its full to-do list application.

Pros and Cons of the digital system

The Pros

You can take it everywhere. When was the last time you left home without your phone? Of course excluding the times you forgot or lost it.

Digital to-do list applications also provide reminders. And that's very useful when you are working on things that have to do with habits. Your paper will never vibrate, or let you know you should do something.

It is sharable. You can't share a piece of paper with other people and still have it. But you can start a task on a to-do list, and sync with other people. That is a very big benefit if you are working with a team at the workplace or somewhere else.

> **The paper system is practically unlimited.**

it offers search functionality. You can easily scour your digital to-do list. For instance, you can easily find something about something you did recently; you won't have to search folders or a file cabinet.

Finally, the digital system of writing to-do lists is a greener solution.

The Cons

It kind of just takes more to input a note in an app. If I want to make a to-do list on something in my paper planner, I just find the right page in my notebook and I am done. But if I am going to do it digitally, I have to break it down and categorize, organize sub notes, and arrange notes for each given task, and so on.

Also, it is too easy to copy and paste tasks. If you are just copying and pasting, it is a lot easier to forget and push tasks to the back of your mind. Lets us say you want to do pushups, and you have been writing it for the past ten days. No doubt, it is a lot easier if you simply copy and paste than you writing on a paper. But on paper, you can physically see what you are writing which makes it easy for you to remember.

The digital to-do list application can just as easily hide a task as it can help you search for hidden tasks. You may have a task under ten subfolders which effectively hides it from your view. On the contrary, with paper, you just need to open up your notebook to find out one thing I should be doing, instead of trying to go through all the different tasks in different sections.

It is distracting. Let's say I want to add a new to-do list on my phone's to-do app. Guess what happens, I get a text message. Where does my mind immediately go? I answer the text message and without knowing, I have just stepped into a conversation. My mind is starting to split. Okay, let's say I go back to my list and as I try to get it done, I get another email straight from my secretary. Where does my mind go? "I just got to go check that right now!"

When you are working with a paper planner you don't have all these wandering distractions. It is very straightforward. You will be able to focus more on the whole planning and production process.

The Crossroads

So, which is better?

Actually, it varies from person to person. I can't say one is better than the other for you. The thing is you must choose for yourself according to your personal preferences and style.. Obviously, there is a different solution suited for different people. The truth is you can't strictly use paper, if your work forces you to use the digital version It is something you just have to accept. But you really have to choose what's better for you.

One thing you should do is to try the paper system for a week.

Get a to-do list book and make a plan for the next week. Don't worry; you don't have to follow through if you don't like it. But the idea is to switch to digital the week after.

When you have tried both, you can decide which system works better for you.

the idea is to switch to digital the week after.

When you have tried both, you can decide which system works better for you.

Prioritize your To-Do List

Whether we are talking about your household chores or your work obligations, prioritizing your to-do list is a powerful and super useful skill that will allow you to tackle your tasks in the best possible way. Prioritizing will ensure that everything that is important will be completed on time. When you prioritize your tasks and shift your focus to the most pressing matters first down to the least important activities, you will reduce how much you have on your plate and will allow yourself to finally breathe.

Before we actually learn how to determine which of your tasks are top priorities and which are not that important, we should first prepare your to-do list for prioritizing:

Choose the Format

Whether you have decided to write your to-do list in a Word document, an Android app, or the old-fashioned way with a pen and paper, one thing is certain – the format you choose has to work for you since you are about to use it regularly.

Your format should include a column for the tasks, a comment box, and a check box where you can check things off when they are completed.

And while a digital format may be way easier to use since it is way simpler and faster for you to reorganize and reprioritize your tasks, rewriting your to-do list by hand can be a great mind tool that will help you focus on the important things and help you remember them better. Just something to think about when choosing however,:it is entirely up to you.

The Breakdown of Priorities

Not every task is the same. Some are of a more pressing nature than others, while some are not even priorities. The point is to choose the level of priority for each task, so you can know which one to complete first. But before we jump into tackling that, we need to see what the priority breakdown should look like.

- Top Priority – These are those tasks that need to be done within the next few hours and are very important.

- Medium Priority – These are those tasks that can wait for tomorrow or even a few more days.

- Low Priority – Important tasks that are not that urgent and can wait for a few days or even weeks.

- Lowest Priority – Something that has to be done, but can wait for weeks or even a few months.

- Nice but not Exactly a Priority – These are those tasks that you want to complete, but are not exactly necessary or a priority. For instance, selling your old laptop (if you don't need the money, of course).

Use Color

Whether using pens in different colors or a highlighter, color can help you easily recognize your priorities in a very neat and clean way. You can underline, highlight, or even change the font color. The important thing is that each of your priorities have a different color in order to distinguish between them. For instance, you can choose to use a yellow highlight for the top priority and underline all of the other priorities with different colors. Really, this is solely up to your own preferences.

Determine What's a Priority

Although deciding what your priorities are may seem like a pretty obvious thing to do, when you are forced to pick no more than ten important tasks at once, choosing where to put your focus first can really be challenging.

Focus on the Problems First

Obviously, the tasks that you should tackle first are the ones that will result in problems without completion, or those that will hurt you in some way. When deciding what exactly is a top priority, think about which task will cause you extreme consequences if you fail to complete them. For instance, let's say that you have these tasks for today:

- Fix the bathroom leak

- Declutter the closet

- Sweep the floor

> **Think about which task will cause you extreme consequences if you fail to complete it.**

It is pretty obvious that "fix the bathroom leak" is a top priority that if left undone, might lead to flooding your home. Sweep the floor may not be as severe, but should be done next since hygiene is a lot more important than closet organization. Use this kind of approach when prioritizing.

Consider the Expectations of Others

Sometimes - especially when there are other people that rely on your input – thinking about what others expect of you and which task they want you to complete, is really important. These people can be your family, boss, coworkers, etc. When prioritizing your tasks, this is also something you should definitely think about. For instance, let's say that your wife has asked you to fix the oven. She is expecting you to tackle this as soon as you get home so she can make dinner. Obviously, this has to be a priority and something that you will take care of as soon as you get back from work.

At work, this is also super important. , If you are working on a project with a couple of other colleagues, that means that your colleagues rely on your input as well. You might have one deadline for the whole project, but your coworkers may also expect that you present your work to them before a certain date. That should be a priority.

Speaking of work, prioritizing in the office is something that most employers and supervisors would expect of you to have mastered by now. Some may even ask interviewees to explain prioritization. As you can see prioritizing tasks matters, and is a highly valued skill to have.

Know How to Shift Your Priorities

Circumstances change. What was a medium priority yesterday, may not be a priority today. Something far more urgent may unexpectedly occur and replace your current top priority. Be prepared for such occurrences and know how to downgrade the task that is of less priority today, and shift your focus to more important things.

If you find it helpful, you can choose to rearrange your master list regularly and prioritize it as well. Eventually, the obvious items such as 'take a shower' should be erased. This is extremely helpful for those people that have long lists that get lost between the set due dates. If setting the deadlines doesn't work for you do some rearranging, where you will be able to simply pick the top 5-10 items to be your daily to-do list, every day.

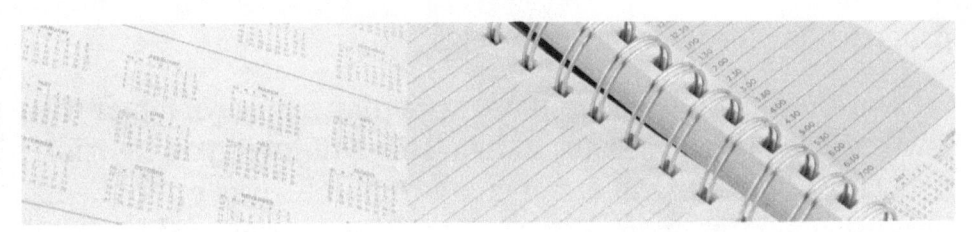

Get Started

Suppose someone calls you for an advice about being overwhelmed. That person might say, "I always have much to do, but I never know where to start, and then I do nothing." What would your response be during this conversation? Would it sound like:" you know what? I used to feel that way too, but I haven't in a couple of years and I am going to share with you what's changed, and what's now happening in my life that I don't experience that problem anymore."

Or you might as well be the victim who needs a bailout for this problem. Well, the good news is I am going to be sharing with you proven methods of selecting a task ahead of time by making an effective to do list.

The biggest thing to remember is why you make to-do lists in the first place, and that is to get the tasks out of your head as well as the associated worries that come with them, and free up that valuable mind of yours to do more important things.

The following is a combination of techniques that I have smashed together to help create a to-do list that really works:

Use Paper for Short-Term Goals

Digital tools, in my opinion, are for planning over long stretches of time, or for planning larger projects. But digital lists have one major disadvantage that makes them really bad for day to day planning; they are never-ending. Give you no idea of how far along you are, whereas a paper list can also be a progress bar for your day.

You should allow yourself no more than a piece of paper with few lines to lay up your to-do list. This will force you to prioritize. Unimportant stuff is not going to find its way on to the list because you simply don't have all the time in the world.

In addition, paper allows the crossing off of items in a much more satisfying way than a digital list, so you could happily move to the next item.

Do some cherry picking

This may probably sound like some kind of lousy advice but trust me, it is magic.

You put something important on your list that you want to do. Maybe it is kind of quick and easy. You should do that item first because the sooner you can cross something off, especially the more important things, the better. You get a rush of dopamine every time you accomplish something, and that is a neurohormone that can in turn, make you more productive. This technique is called priming.

You don't need to finish the list.

Now at first, it seems to fly right in the face of something I mentioned earlier, which is that your list is your progress bar for your day. So how would you not feel like a total failure when you only get two things done on your list in a day? You do what I do. You look at that incomplete list and you don't let it discourage you.

Ultimately you can only do as much as you can do in one day, no matter how long your list is.

Efficiently and effectively making your next list

Whenever you need to start a new list, move the items that

are important and leave the ones that are not. This is a good time to decide what items are falling into the realm of unimportant, and simply don't do them. Now we have a nice shiny new list with only important items in them.

Let us go on to what may be the most important tip of all.

Draw little boxes with shadows.

As you are making a list, draw a little box next to each major item, a little empty checkbox. And then, when you are finishing up the list, go back to each box and then draw a little drop shadow.

Drawing a little drop shadow is a peaceful sort of mini-meditation exercise. It is pretty focusing and calming, and it has three little bonuses:

First, there is the application of the dopamine rush that comes with crossing items off, because now you have to check little boxes too.

Secondly, when you enter into this meditative state, it will give your mind time to focus, and subconsciously deal with the items on that list.

Thirdly, like clockwork, when you are in this state, new and important items will come into your head.

Rules of Compilation

The fact that you have decided to create a to-do list is nothing but good news. But if you think that you can just sit down, list all of the tasks that you should do, and then jump on the productivity bandwagon, you couldn't be more wrong. Despite its name, writing a to-do list doesn't really mean listing everything that you need to do and create a lengthy, novel-like list that will be too exhausting to even look at, let alone go through it and cross the completed tasks out.

There is no point in writing a to-do list if you are going to let it overwhelm you. The right to-do list has to be a motivation booster, and in order to be one, it has to:

1. Fit Into Your Goals

2. Be Personal

3. Be Well-Crafted

Now that you know why your current to-do list isn't working and have decided to turn a new leaf and set up another one, here is what you should know to write the ultimate to-do list.

It Has to Fit Into Your Goals

Obviously, the more excited you are about something, the more you want to do it. If you are excited about the tasks listed in your to-do lists, you will have no problem in completing them.

Each and every item in your to-do list has to have meaning

to you and be a part of a certain dream or goal of yours. That is the best and only way to ensure that you will stay motivated and on the right track.

One of the best methods to ensure motivation is to think about how each task from your list connects to your goals. So, before you start listing items in your to-do list, ask yourself "What do I want to accomplish?" "Are my tasks and obligations somehow a part of my goals?"

Think about the tasks that you need to complete and how they are connected to your goals. How is buying milk going to get you to your goals? Be specific.

> **Each and every item in your to-do list has to have a meaning to you and be a part of a certain dream or goal of yours.**

Let's say that you are a working mother. Perhaps your goals in life are to make your kids happy, to enjoy time with your family, to provide for your family, to write a book, to travel somewhere new each year, to be in a good shape, etc.

Start looking at each task as a stepping stone that leads to your goals. For instance, maybe buying milk is a task that will lead to making cookies and making your kids happy. Perhaps, taking your shirt to the dry cleaners can be an opportunity for you to walk a mile, which will contribute to your goal of being in good shape.

Of course, these are just examples. You will have to find the link between your tasks and goals on your own. The point is to find the motivation trigger behind every chore and obligation.

It Has to be Personal

As much as crafting a to-do list properly can help you increase your productivity, and make your list fit into your goals, sometimes this will just not be enough.

First of all, keep in mind that we are all different. What works for me may not work for your life and schedule. That's why your to-do list has to be personal. I am telling you this before revealing to you the secrets of creating a successful list, because I believe that if you take a personal approach from the very beginning, you will be a lot more successful at crossing the tasks out.

5. So please, before you grab your pen and paper (or your smartphone), ask yourself what can be accomplished and what can't. I know how overwhelming this may be, so I'm going to give you a helping hand.

It Has to Be Well-Crafted

It is of great importance that you craft and organize your activities in a way that will work and bring productivity. Once you create your to-do list with the tips from below (next chapter), you will never have more on your plate than you can handle.

Ten strategies of building the to-do list

This is where the rubber meets the road. We're going to take everything we've covered thus far and use it to build an effective to-do list system.

The system we're about to create will make it easier for you to get your most important work done on time. It will reduce your stress, eliminate your frustration, and help you to focus and avoid distractions along the way.

Most people underestimate the importance of their to-do lists. They misjudge the impact their lists will have on their productivity. As you read the following sections, I encourage you to take the opposite view. Recognize that your to-do list plays a vital role in how your day progresses. An effective system will not only help you to stay on top of your workflow, but will also help you manage your daily life.

Let's build the perfect to-do list.

Step 1: Isolate Current Tasks From Future Tasks

First, use a "current task" list to decide how to allocate your time and attention each day. This list will carry the to-do items that must be completed before the day ends.

Second, use a "future task" list to keep track of all the items that will need your attention at some point. You won't use this list during the course of your workday. Instead, you'll refer to it at the end of the day to create the following day's to-do list.

This simple step, separating current tasks from future tasks, is critical. It can mean the difference between getting high-value work done on time and becoming overwhelmed under a mountain of tasks with varying priorities and deadlines.

Many people work from a single, massive to-do list that grows by the day as new items are added to it. This practice can be discouraging because there's no end in sight. Those who work in this manner never manage to get through their lists, so they always feel as if they're merely treading water.

Separating current and future tasks short-circuits this feeling. The massive list, the one that contains all future tasks, is set aside. No attention is paid to it during the workday. In its stead, the current task list takes the spotlight. Its limited scope - remember, it only carries items that are to be completed that day - reduces stress and removes the sense of anxiety.

This is a slight deviation from the "next actions" list used in GTD. That list doesn't limit your focus to the current day. As such, the "next actions" list could potentially go on for several pages.

This is a crucial distinction. You'll find that completing each day's to-do list will motivate and inspire you. There's something invigorating about crossing off every item from your list. You'll feel as if the day is a productive success.

Imagine experiencing that positive feeling day after day.

Step 2: Define Tasks By Desired Outcomes

The only reason to do something is if doing it moves you closer toward achieving a specific goal. For example, few people study calculus in their free time. Most do so in order to complete schoolwork, prepare for a test, or broaden their skill set.

Likewise, few people clean out their rain gutters for enjoyment. They do so to prevent water damage to their roofs.

We take action to effect specific outcomes. Otherwise, why would we spend time and effort doing things that prevent us from pursuing activities we find more enjoyable (for example, binge-watching our favorite TV series on Netflix)?

Consider that notion in the context of your to-do lists. How often have you failed to complete tasks - or even start working on them - because they appeared to have little importance to you? Chances are the tasks weren't attached to specific goals you wanted to achieve.

The simplest way to get through your daily to-do list is to assign a "why" to each item found on it. Know the reason the item is on your list. Determine why you need to get it done. Write the reason down next to the task.

For example, suppose your to-do list carries the item "call my parents." You probably have a reason to call them, if only to check in and see how they're doing. Alternatively, you might want to invite them to breakfast or ask them about a family-related matter.

The point is, calling your parents is intended to accomplish a specific goal. Write down that goal, or desired outcome, next to the task. You'll be more likely to follow through on it if you see the reason for doing it.

It's not enough to keep the reasons for doing tasks in your head. You must write them down. Doing so makes it material. A reason written down is more real than a reason bouncing around in your head.

You'll find that when you associate tasks with specific outcomes, you'll feel more compelled to get them done. Taking action will signify progress toward goals you hope to achieve - goals that are important to you.

This is one of the defining traits of an effective to-do list.

Step 3: Break Projects Down To Individual Tasks

You've probably heard this joke: How do you eat an elephant? One bite at a time. It illustrates an important concept related to task management. The only way to complete any project is to first break it down to its constituent parts. A project is moved forward by working on the individual tasks that are incumbent to its completion.

You know this intuitively. But do you apply the principle to your daily to-do lists?

When we're faced with a large project, it's difficult to know where to begin. Consequently, we become more prone to distractions. Any distraction is preferable to grappling with an endeavor for which we lack direction and momentum.

This is the reason many to-do "items" remain unfinished at the end of the day. They're technically projects that are too large in scope and can seem overwhelming, which causes us to procrastinate. We ultimately carry them forward to the following day, where they continue to haunt us.

If we don't invest the time to break down projects to their smaller, more manageable pieces, this motivation-crushing process is likely to repeat itself day after day.

Let's look at an example.

Suppose one of the items on your master list is "clean the house." This is a project, one that can potentially take hours to complete. Listed as a single item, it's overwhelming. It's difficult to know where to start.

So let's break down the project to smaller tasks, each of which offers focus and can be completed in less time. Here's a starter list:

- Wash the dishes
- Clean the kitchen countertops

- Mop the kitchen floor
- Clean the downstairs bathroom
- Clean the upstairs bathrooms
- Vacuum the floors
- Dust the furniture

Notice that each of the above tasks is actionable and more importantly, each one is independent of the others. You don't have to address them in any particular order.

This gives you flexibility in how you schedule time to complete the tasks. Rather than setting aside four hours to "clean the house," you can set aside 10 minutes to wash the dishes, 15 minutes to mop the kitchen floor, and 30 minutes to clean the downstairs bathroom.

Breaking projects down into smaller tasks makes them seem more doable. It also allows you to focus your limited time and attention on tasks according to their priority and value. For example, washing the dishes may be a high-priority item that warrants your immediate attention. Meanwhile, vacuuming the floors can be postponed until tomorrow without consequence.

It's important to make the distinction.

Make sure your to-do lists are limited to actionable tasks, not projects. If an item requires more than one action, it is a project that can - and should - be broken down. By breaking them down, you'll enjoy better focus and get important work done more quickly.

Step 4: Assign A Deadline To Each Task

You already know the importance of deadlines. They help us to focus our time and attention on important tasks. They help us to organize our calendars. They encourage us to take action. Studies also show they improve our performance.

Ultimately, deadlines increase our efficiency and productivity, spurring us to get important stuff done.

For this reason, every task on your master to-do list should have a deadline associated with it. The date doesn't have to be written in stone. It can change as the priority and urgency of the task to which it's attached changes.

> One of the most common problems with to-do lists is that they're too long.

Nor must the date be precise. Your task list may include to-do items that need to be addressed at some point, but can be put on the back burner for now. A due date of "mid-June," rather than "June 14," may suffice if the task isn't due for several months.

Attaching a deadline to every item on your master to-do list makes it easier to know which tasks to select for your daily to-do list. You can tell at a glance which items need your attention tomorrow and which ones can be shelved until a future date.

Having said that, it's not enough to assign a deadline to each item. The manner in which you do so is equally important. It will influence your morale, motivation, and ability to focus. Your strategy in setting deadlines will dictate whether they are effective.

Here are a few tips...

First, make sure each deadline is realistic.

Second, come up with a reason for each due date.

Third, give yourself less time than you think you need.

Step 5: Limit The Number Of Current Tasks To Seven

One of the most common problems with to-do lists is that they're too long. Those that start with just a few tasks invariably grow to include dozens. It's no wonder so many people are unable to get through their to-do lists. Doing so is practically impossible!

On the one hand, this circumstance is understandable. During the course of any given day, new projects are conceived and new tasks are born from them.

But that doesn't mean you should add them to your daily task list. In fact, doing so would be setting yourself up for failure.

I strongly recommend limiting the number of items on your daily to-do list to seven. This is a manageable number. Assuming no single task requires hours to complete, it's possible to get through your entire list by the end of the day.

Step 6: Organize Tasks By Project, Type, Or Location

It's common to treat the master task list as a rolling "brain dump." New tasks are added to the bottom of the list as you think of them. The problem is, if you leave it in that condition, it will eventually become overwhelming.

Even if you give each item a deadline and provide various types of context, your list will become burdensome over time. You'll find it increasingly difficult to manage tasks. A lot of items will end up falling through the cracks.

Imagine reviewing 20 pages of to-do items. My own master list used to be much longer before I learned how to create effective lists. Finding specific tasks and managing the associated projects took too much time.

No longer. I now organize tasks based on various contexts: by project, type, and location. I maintain multiple lists accordingly. (Note that these lists are separate and distinct from my daily to-do list.)

Task-level context is an important part of any to-do list system. It defines how long items should take to complete. It reminds you of the reasons to get them done. It encourages you to focus on tasks that have the highest priorities given your goals.

For these reasons, categorize each task on your master to-do list using the following three contexts:

1. Project
2. Type
3. Location

I recommend creating a separate list for each project, each type of task, and each location. For example, the following projects would warrant their own lists:

- Write a book
- Remodel my kitchen
- Buy a car

The following types of tasks would also warrant their own lists:

- Analytical work
- Creative work
- Mindless work

Likewise, the following locations would warrant their own lists:

- At the office
- At home
- On the road

Categorizing to-do items by project, type, and location will keep you organized. It will also help you to choose tasks for your daily list that complement your circumstances.

For example, "vacuum the living room" is clearly a location-based task. You must be at home to do it. If you plan to be at the office all day, you wouldn't add this item to your daily list.

Some tasks can - and should - be assigned to more than one context.

For example, consider the project "Write a Book." One of your early tasks is to "write the first draft of chapter 1." This task is already categorized by project. But if the only time you're able to write is while you're at home, it should also be categorized by location. Moreover, keep in mind that writing is creative work that requires mental energy. As such, it may be useful to categorize it by type of activity. That way, you can schedule it on your calendar for times when your energy levels are high.

If you're creating to-do lists on paper, assigning multiple contexts to tasks can be problematic. One solution is to color code them.

For example, the task "write the first draft of chapter 1" is already found under the project "write a book." Color-coding for that context is unnecessary. But you can use colored pens to assign location and activity type contexts. Red can signify "at home" and blue can signify "creative work."

This is an imperfect solution, of course. A better approach is to use an online tool, such as "Todoist." It offers tagging and labeling features with a palette of colors that make it easy to organize to-do items by multiple contexts.

One last note before we move on. You may find it useful to keep a separate list for high-priority, high-value to-do items. Some people call this a HIT list, or high-impact task list.

Personally, I find the use of a HIT list to be overkill. I already assign a priority to every item on my various lists. Creating an additional list for high-impact items is unnecessary. It hampers my efficiency rather than improve it.

But I wanted to mention the practice in the event you find it helps your workflow. Remember, this is about creating a system that works for you.

Step 7: Rid Your List Of Unnecessary Tasks

One of the most important things you can do is to keep your master to-do list clean. You need to prune the list on a regular basis, purging tasks that are no longer necessary or consistent with your goals. Otherwise, it can quickly become unmanageable as you add new items to it each day.

Pruning your list helps you to keep it under control. You'll be able to more easily identify important projects and their associated tasks. Task management is made simpler when irrelevant items are removed, or crossed off your list.

Pruning also increases your efficiency. It limits your master list to tasks that advance your most important work. Consequently, you won't waste valuable time and attention on nonessential activities.

What types of tasks are candidates for removal? Look for these four items:

1. Wishes
2. Unclear tasks
3. Trivial tasks
4. Resolutions

Wishes are typically phrased as projects rather than actionable tasks. For example, you might wish to "remodel your kitchen." You may wish to "take your family to Kauai next summer." Wishes are overly broad in scope and rarely essential to achieving well-defined goals. As such, they should be removed from your master to-do list.

Keep these items on a wish list.

Unclear tasks are those that lack context. You'll sometimes find they're in that state because they don't warrant your attention. They hang in limbo until you notice them.

An example would be to "call John." Why do you need to call John? How will doing so move your important work forward? Are there consequences if you fail to make the call? If so, what are they?

If a task on your master list is unclear, reevaluate its value in light of your goals. It may be a good candidate for removal.

Trivial tasks can be eliminated without repercussions. These are random items that are recorded when they surface, and promptly forgotten. Your master list will accumulate them. That's its purpose - to clear your head of things that are difficult to remember and organize. But you'll find that, under closer examination, many of these items can - and should be - removed from the list.

Resolutions are promises. They differ from normal to-do items because they typically require a change in habit. For example, you might resolve to "exercise," "lose weight," or "learn Spanish." It's fine to have such goals, of course. But don't confuse them with actionable tasks.

Remove all resolutions from your master to-do list. They don't belong there. Instead, put them on a separate "lifestyle goals" list and treat them as projects. Then, when you're ready to act on one of them, create a separate list for it. Break it down to small, actionable tasks and assign deadlines.

A large, cumbersome master to-do list is discouraging. If you allow it to grow unchecked, it can slowly erode your motivation and crush your creativity. Keep it clean by regularly pruning unnecessary tasks. Doing so will make your list feel much alive because every task on it will have a specific purpose.

With periodic pruning, you'll be able to more easily identify important tasks for your daily to-do lists. You'll also spend less time on insignificant items, greatly increasing your productivity along the way.

Step 8: Estimate The Amount Of Time Each Task Will Take To Complete

You should know how long each to-do item on your master list will take you to finish. This information allows you to choose tasks for your daily list based on how much time you'll have available to work on them. If you know each task's estimated completion time, you can create realistic to-do lists. You can avoid saddling yourself with tasks that need to be carried over to the next day.

Most people neglect to take this step. Sadly, it's one of the most damaging omissions they can make. It can mean the difference between getting through their to-do lists and feeling frustrated and overwhelmed by them at the end of the day.

In order to calculate a task's estimated completion time, you must know what is required to do the task. This includes tools, information, and input from others.

For example, suppose one of the tasks on your to-do list is to "finish the accounts receivable report for the boss." In order to complete the report, you may need input from your company's sales department. You might also need to refer to last week's accounts receivable and cash flow reports. How long will it take you to obtain the necessary information and resources? These requirements should be taken into account when estimating the task's completion time.

Review your master list and assign a time estimate to each item. Whether the item will take 15 minutes or 3 hours, write down the estimate next to it.

Resist the temptation to guess. We tend to be overly optimistic regarding our ability to get things done. We underestimate the time we need. Be aware of this tendency.

Come up with a realistic estimate based on the resources you'll need (including input from others) and the challenges you're likely to encounter along the way.

If you're familiar with the task, you'll know what resources you need and how much time it will take to complete it. You'll be able to assign a reasonably accurate estimate. If you're unfamiliar with the task, talk to someone who has worked on it in the past. Ask that person how much time it usually takes him or her.

As you assign estimated completion times to the to-do items on your master list, you'll face an interesting conundrum. I noted above that we tend to underestimate the amount of time we'll need to complete tasks. We're inclined to be overly optimistic. However, we also tend to give ourselves too much time to get things done.

For example, take mowing the lawn. Suppose a realistic completion time is 45 minutes. In our optimism, we convince ourselves that we can finish the job in under 30 minutes. Yet, because there's no urgency behind the task, we give ourselves an hour and a half.

Step 9: Lead Each Task With An Active Verb

Sometimes, all you need is the right word to spur you to action. Verbs have that power. Put them in front of your to-do items and you'll be more inclined to get the items done.

When you phrase a task with a verb, the task comes alive. It goes from being a mere line item on your to-do list to being an actionable assignment. The verb triggers something in the brain, prompting it to focus on completing the item.

Let's take a look at a few examples. Following are "tasks" (technically, they're little more than notes) that lack verbs:

- Laundry
- Sandra's birthday cake
- Accounts receivable report
- Car tires
- Breakfast with parents

Notice how the tasks lack emotional and motivational power. We can fix that by adding verbs to them:

- Start a load of laundry
- Buy a cake for Sandra's birthday
- Finish the accounts receivable report
- Check the pressure in my car's tires
- Call parents to plan breakfast date

Notice how the verbs (start, buy, finish, check, and call) tell us exactly what to do. There's no ambiguity. You don't have to guess at the type of activity the task involves. The verb defines it.

Also, notice how the verbs make it easier to estimate task completion times. It's difficult to know how long the task "laundry" will take. But you can "start a load of laundry" in five minutes.

Not just any verb will do. There's an art to choosing the right ones. The key is to be specific.

The right verbs encourage execution. They encourage you to take action. The wrong ones do the opposite. They encourage procrastination. Verbs like explore, plan, and touch base lack specificity. As a result, they're less effective than verbs like research, draft, and call. These latter choices have more impact because they imply specific actions. They leave nothing open to interpretation.

Phrasing tasks with the right action verbs will motivate you to take action on them. You'll be less susceptible to distractions and less likely to procrastinate because you'll know exactly what you need to do.

The result? You'll get through your daily to-do lists more quickly, getting more done in less time.

Step 10: Note Which Tasks Require Input From Others

Some of the tasks on your daily to-do list will require input from other people. For example, you might be working on a team-based project and need certain team members to complete specific tasks before you can address the ones for which you're responsible.

Even if you're working alone, others' input may be vital to your workflow. For instance, the accounts receivable report you've been tasked to complete might require input from someone in your sales department. The conference call you intend to hold may require information you've asked a co-worker to obtain for you.

It's important to know, at a glance, which items on your task list require action from other people. Write a short note next to each to-do item for which you're waiting for someone's input. Detail the type of input you need, its format (email, phone call, report, spreadsheet, etc.), and the date you expect it to be delivered.

The expected delivery date will prompt you to follow up with the person if you don't receive his or her input in a timely fashion. To that end, it will help you to set expectations for others and hold them accountable for needed deliveries This is critical if your workflow depends on them taking action.

Most people neglect to take this step. They fail to make notes regarding their need for input from other parties. Unfortunately, if their workflow depends on others, this omission will ruin their estimates concerning the time needed to complete tasks. They'll end up spending valuable time in limbo, waiting for other people to act. This, of course, will hobble their ability to get things done, severely impacting their productivity.

Conclusion

Never underestimate the power of a to-do list. We live in a fast-paced, information-overloaded world, and sometimes it feels like we're being pulled in a million different directions. One of the reasons we're stressed out is because our minds are filled with incomplete thoughts and ideas. My suggestion is to stop thinking about them and start creating lists to guide your actions.

Moreover, to-do lists help evaluate the importance of a specific idea. If you find that you're continuously procrastinating or not taking action, then it's a sign that the task is not aligned with a personal goal. If you put an item on a list that's reviewed on a daily basis, you'll quickly figure out if it's really worth pursuing.

Lastly, I feel a to-do list allows you to clarify every thought that pops into your head. Getting great ideas is a commonplace experience, but it's a whole other ballgame to turn a random thought into an actionable plan, and then into a completed project. With a to-do list, you can map out every step of a process and turn it into a daily action plan.

It's okay if you make mistakes along the way. That's how we all learn those important lessons in life.

www.ingramcontent.com/pod-product-compliance
Lightning Source LLC
Chambersburg PA
CBHW030524220526
45463CB00007B/2711